Everyday PLAY

Fun Games to Develop the Fine Motor Skills Your Child Needs for School

Christy Isbell

Gryphon House
Silver Spring, MD

Published by Gryphon House, Inc.
10770 Columbia Pike, Suite 201, Silver Spring, MD 20901
800.638.0928; 301.595.9500; 301.595.0051 (fax)

Visit us on the web at www.gryphonhouse.com

Illustrations: Chris Wold Dyrud

Library of Congress Cataloging-in-Publication Information:
Isbell, Christy.
 Everyday play / by Christy Isbell ; illustrated by Chris Wold Dyrud ; photographs by Christy Isbell.
    p. cm.
 ISBN 978-0-87659-125-3
 1. Motor ability in children. 2. Left- and right-handedness. 3. Play.
 I. Title.
 BF723.M6I83 2010
 155.4'1235--dc22
                   2009044841

Bulk purchase
Gryphon House books are available for special premiums and sales promotions as well as for fund-raising use. Special editions or book excerpts also can be created to specification. For details, contact the Director of Marketing at Gryphon House.

Disclaimer
Gryphon House, Inc. and the author cannot be held responsible for damage, mishap, or injury incurred during the use of or because of activities in this book. Appropriate and reasonable caution and adult supervision of children involved in activities and corresponding to the age and capability of each child involved is recommended at all times. Do not leave children unattended at any time. Observe safety and caution at all times.

Table of Contents

Chapter 1
The Finer Points of Fine Motor Play

Your child is naturally curious. One of the ways he learns about the world is by exploring objects and materials with his hands. These hand skills are called fine motor skills. During the early years, your child learns to use his hands for important skills, such as feeding and dressing himself, as well as for play, work, and self-care skills he will need for the rest of his life. As a responsive parent, you help establish your child's sense of trust and security; a child who feels nurtured and supported is more likely to try new things. This book will help you understand and observe how children develop fine motor skills, and how you can join in your child's everyday play to help him grow in new directions.

Your child uses her fine motor skills when she is at home, at school, and in the community. At home, she may use her hands to eat dry cereal, feed herself with a spoon or fork, drink from a cup, zip up her coat, snap her pants, or unbutton her shirt. At preschool, your child may use her hands to clap along with music, do fingerplays, put on dress-up clothes, wash a doll, build with blocks, draw, cut with scissors, or put together puzzles. Your child may use her fine motor skills in a variety of ways when she is out and about in her environment. She may use her hands to push the button on an elevator, open plastic bags of snacks, turn on a faucet, and wash her hands.

You can build those skills every day by playing the games and doing the activities in this book. Now is the time for playful learning.

What Fine Motor Skills Should My Preschooler Learn?

By the time your child is six years old, she should be able to perform the following basic fine motor actions:

- **Reach**: Move her arm forward to grasp or touch an object.
- **Grasp**: Use her fingers to get an object into her hand.
- **Carry**: Use her hand to move an object from one place to another place.
- **Release**: Let go of an object she holds in her hand.
- **In-hand Manipulation**: Use her fingers to adjust an object inside her hand.
- **Bilateral Hand Use**: Use her two hands together in an activity.

How Can I Help My Preschooler Develop Fine Motor Skills?

Give your child a wide variety of materials to explore in new and different ways. Paper, pens, markers, crayons, glue, clay, and small blocks spark your child's imagination and invite her to create things that are interesting to her. She will enjoy this open-ended exploration and, at the same time, it will help her develop her fine motor skills.

When you and your child do the fine motor activities in this book, remember that the product of the activity is not as important as the process. Giving your four-year-old child a blank piece of paper, a choice of several different paintbrushes, and a set of watercolor paints will provide more interesting ways for him to practice his fine motor skills than offering him a coloring book and crayons.

When your child is learning to use a new tool such as an eyedropper or a hole punch, show her the proper and safest method to use these tools.

Keep your instructions simple and brief. Clearly demonstrate the basic ways to use the tool or material, and then give her time to explore how she can use the tool.

Before you begin an activity, talk to your child about safety precautions. Generally, one or two "safety tips" are all that your child will be able to remember. Simply explain how your child can use the tool or material safely. Here are some examples:

> We use a stapler to staple paper together.
> Watch your fingers! Keep them on top of the stapler.
> We use scissors at the table.

Several factors may influence your child's fine motor development, including muscle tone, body build, temperament, and even gender. Frequently, girls are more competent than boys of the same age at performing fine motor activities, such as drawing, handwriting, and cutting with scissors. Every child will develop fine motor skills at her own pace.

The Foundations of Fine Motor Skills

Here is a list of the foundations necessary for fine motor skills:

Developmental Readiness: Building, stacking, and putting things together fascinate young children. Preschoolers begin to understand shapes and sizes and begin to differentiate between the "part" and the "whole." Activities that give your child the opportunity to build and construct using blocks and other similar objects will help him become developmentally ready to participate in activities such as drawing, cutting, and stringing beads.

Good Posture/Balance: Fine motor activities are easier to complete when a child sits with her feet firmly on the floor and with her back straight.

Your child should be able to use her arms to manipulate objects rather than using them to hold herself steady at the table.

Shoulder Strength: Your child's shoulder strength provides a stable base of support for his hand function. Young children who do not regularly participate in large motor activities such as climbing, crawling, pushing, and pulling may not develop good upper-body strength.

Grasp: Your child should be able to hold a writing tool (for example, a crayon, marker, or pencil) before you begin helping her learn pre-writing skills. The grasp ought to be strong enough that your child can hold the writing tool, but flexible enough to allow her to move the tool across a paper surface. Most three-year-olds hold a crayon with all of their fingers, and the majority of five-year-olds use their thumb, index, and middle fingers to hold the crayon. By the time your child reaches first grade she should have a mature grasp.

Forearm and Wrist Control: Your child should be able to swivel his forearm so that his palm is up and then down. Your child's ability to hold his wrist firm while moving his fingers is particularly important for activities such as cutting and lacing or stringing. These skills will improve dramatically between ages three and five.

Bilateral Hand Use: Using two hands together to complete an activity is essential for success in fine motor activities. By age three, your child should learn to stabilize an object with one hand and move her other hand. For example, she should be able to hold down a piece of paper with one hand and draw on that paper with her other hand. By age five, your child should begin developing **reciprocal hand use.** This means she can cut with one hand and turn the paper with the other hand to create large, simple shapes.

Eye-Hand Coordination: Your child needs to develop strong interaction between his visual and hand skills. He needs to be able to use his vision to coordinate the movement of his shoulders, elbows, wrists, and fingers as he learns to use a new tool or participates in a new fine motor activity.

Writing

In addition to the foundations of good fine motor skills, your child must be able to scribble independently on paper before beginning pre-writing activities. Most young children follow this progression:

- Copy a horizontal line.
- Copy a vertical line.
- Copy a circle.
- Copy a cross.
- Copy a right-to-left diagonal.
- Copy a square.
- Copy a left-to-right diagonal.
- Copy an "X."
- Copy a triangle.
- Copy a diamond.

Note: "Copy" here means that the child can look at a picture or drawing of a particular form, and without a demonstration of how to make the line or shape, be able to create an imitation of the drawing.

In general, this progression begins sometime around age two. Most children will be able to copy a triangle and a diamond by the time they are four-and-a-half years old. Once your child can copy all forms and shapes, she should be ready to begin writing letters.

When It Comes to Writing, Don't Rush It

Your child should spend more time playing with manipulatives than practicing writing skills. Avoid the temptation to begin formal handwriting, such as making specific letters, before your child is developmentally ready. If you push your child to write before his hands are physically ready, he may become less interested in writing. In addition, practicing these higher-level fine motor skills before your child is ready puts him at risk for developing poor pencil grasp, illegible handwriting, and slow handwriting (see page 121).

Developmental Steps for Learning How to Write

Your child will learn pre-writing skills best by playing and by taking part in daily life activities. The developmental steps that children typically follow in learning to write are below.

Modeling/Imitating: You show your child how to draw a line or shape, and your child imitates it.

Tracing: Your child traces over a line or shape. Some children are able to skip the tracing step, as they will be able to copy a shape after modeling/imitating.

Copying: The child looks at the completed line or shape and copies it.

Creating: The child creates her own lines and shapes.

The time that each child spends in each developmental step varies. Each time your child attempts a new form or shape, he will most likely need to go through these same steps. Expose your child to a wide variety of print (for example books, magazines, and cards), art, environmental designs (for example traffic signs or labels), and markers, crayons or pencils during play so that he will have many opportunities to imitate and model pre-writing.

By age four, many children will spend more time creating shapes and drawings of their own and less time imitating and tracing. During this stage, engaging in open-ended activities that use blank paper and various writing tools will allow your child to practice her new pre-writing skills. Labeling a child's drawing or writing her story on paper is a great way to demonstrate letter formation.

Some children are ready to begin writing at age five. Most children will start by writing their first names. Some children will be interested in writing letters that are not in their names and may begin to participate in inventive spelling. The best way to promote your child's handwriting skills is to provide a literacy-rich environment that includes a variety of opportunities for him to observe, attempt, and master pre-writing activities first and then follow with letter-writing activities.

Cutting

Your child will follow these general developmental stages of learning to use scissors:

- Hold scissors appropriately (one hand, thumb on top).
- Open and close scissors.
- Snip paper.
- Cut forward through a sheet of paper.
- Cut in a straight line.
- Cut out a square or triangle.
- Cut out a circle.
- Cut non-paper material (such as yarn, tape, or fabric).

Note: A child begins by cutting large simple shapes and progresses to cutting smaller shapes.

This sequence typically begins when children are about two-and-a-half years old. Many young children first attempt to hold scissors with their thumbs down or using two hands.

By age three, your child may be able to hold a sheet of paper in one hand and manipulate the scissors in her other hand to snip the paper. By age five-and-a-half, she may be able to cut out simple shapes and use scissors to cut non-paper materials for creative activities.

These descriptions of how children develop their writing and scissor skills are guidelines. Each child will have his own interest and skill level. As a result, children will progress through the sequences differently as they develop these fine motor skills.

Making Room for Fine Motor Fun

You may want to designate a small area in your home where your child can explore fine motor play. Your fine motor learning space may be a small area or corner of a room. This space will work best in a spot where the floors are easy to clean. If your entire floor is carpeted, you may want to cover the floor with a shower curtain or sheet to protect surfaces.

Once you've decided where to set up the space, begin collecting objects and materials that will stimulate your child's fine motor development. See the list of developmentally appropriate materials and tools for your child to use (on pages 18–20) for suggestions. Stock the area with the right materials and welcome your child into her new space.

Now it's time to play! Simply find the chapter that matches your child's developmental level and choose the activities you think he will enjoy. Have fun, be a good observer, and enjoy this amazing time of growth and development with your child.

Chapter 2
Just the "Write" Size: Selecting Fine Motor Tools and Materials

Give your child the right tools and materials that provide the "just right challenge." A tool that is too difficult for your child to manipulate may discourage him and he may give up. An activity that is too simple for your child may cause your child to quickly lose interest in the task.

Preschoolers work best with tools that fit easily into their small hands. Select tools that will make it easy for a child to be successful so that the she can see her hard work pay off. For example, plastic scissors may appear to be a safe and appropriate option for some children, but plastic scissors are difficult to use when cutting thin paper. Using plastic scissors may frustrate your child. Being a careful observer as you watch your child play will help you gauge her interest level and skill and modify the activity so she can be successful.

The "Write" Stuff

Writing and Drawing Utensils: Your child's grasp of a writing utensil is important because it has an impact on your child's handwriting skill. By the end of kindergarten, most children will have established a particular method for grasping their writing tools. These grasps are habit-based and are very difficult to change once a child practices it long enough. Using the appropriate size and type of writing utensil will help your child develop and practice an efficient pencil grasp that will carry over into elementary school.

For three-year-olds or inexperienced preschoolers, provide large writing tools, such as thick chalk, pencils, crayons, and paintbrushes; bulb paintbrushes; and easy-grip (round-top) crayons. These "thick" utensils are easier for children to grasp in their small hands. Large markers are especially effective for beginning writers because large markers move smoothly across the paper and are easy to hold.

Some four-year-olds and most five-year-olds have developed enough foundational skills for writing that they are ready to use standard-sized writing utensils. Adult-sized pencils, golf pencils, thin markers, and small paintbrushes will encourage a more effective grasp. This means children will start to hold the writing tool with fewer fingers, as well as start to separate their thumb and index finger while writing. Do not throw away short pencils and broken crayons; use them to help a more mature preschooler use his thumb, index, and middle finger to grasp a pencil.

Scissors: Small, round-tipped scissors are typically the best choice for preschoolers. Select scissors that have small holes for a young child's fingers and that are not longer than 5". School-style scissors, which both right- or left-handed children can use, work well. Make sure that the scissors are sharp enough to cut paper easily and open and close smoothly.

Cutting Materials: For beginning or less-skilled cutters, use heavyweight paper, such as index cards, magazine inserts or junk-mail cards, construction paper, or paper bags. Heavier paper is less floppy, more stable, and will allow the child more control for cutting.

Playdough is another heavy material that works well for snipping with scissors. Preschoolers with a moderate skill level can cut regular-weight paper. More advanced preschoolers may cut light-weight materials, such as foil, wax paper, and tissue paper. Non-paper items, such as yarn and fabric, are the most challenging to cut—save these until your child is skilled at cutting regular paper.

Glue: Large glue sticks may be easier for young preschoolers to hold in their hands. More experienced preschoolers can use smaller glue sticks that can apply glue to the surface more accurately. Dipping craft sticks or cotton swabs into a small container of glue (for example, a small paper cup) may be useful for some activities. Once your preschooler develops enough hand strength to squeeze with control, she can begin to squeeze school glue bottles in fine motor activities, which is a great way for her to build hand strength.

Stringing/Lacing: Stringing and lacing activities require good eye-hand coordination. Typically, young children learn to string objects first. Once they are confident in their stringing abilities, children are often more willing to attempt lacing activities, such as lacing cards or boards. When selecting materials for stringing or lacing, consider the size of the holes in the object and the length of the hard tip of the string or lace. For young preschoolers, it helps to start stringing objects that have large holes and that the children can hold easily. String that is stiff and has a long, hard tip will be easier for small hands to manipulate. Rope with duct tape stabilizing the end, thick shoelaces, or long straws also work well. As your child develops more skill, he can begin stringing very small objects, such as small jewelry beads, onto plastic string or thread.

Table and Chair: A sturdy table and a chair that is the appropriate height are important. A chair should allow the young child's knees to bend at a 90° angle. When your child is sitting in the chair, she should be able to place her feet firmly on the ground. The table should be a height that allows the child's elbows to bend and rest lightly on the tabletop. Placing a telephone book or box under your child's feet is a simple way to provide your child with the necessary balancing support. Standing at a table is another good way for your child to develop her sense of balance as she completes various fine motor activities.

Vertical Surfaces: Writing on vertical surfaces—such as an easel—will help your child develop a good grasp and learn the appropriate wrist position for drawing and writing. Three-year-olds should draw or paint on a vertical surface every day. Drawing on a vertical surface tends to encourage the proper formation of shapes and letters.

If you do not have an easel in your home, let your child use a sturdy 3" three-ring binder as a table-top easel or set up a binder for your child to use while lying on the floor (see instructions on page 71). Another simple solution is to tape or clip paper to the wall to create a vertical drawing and writing surface.

Low-Cost, High-Impact Materials and Tools

In most fine motor activities, it is a good idea to use materials that are cost effective and environmentally friendly. Materials such as old newspaper, magazines, and greeting cards can be effectively re-used in fun and interesting ways. With the appropriate tools and materials, young children are more likely to develop self-confidence and a sense of pride about achieving independence in the particular fine motor activity. Here are some items to use with your preschooler at home:

- Individual chalk board and eraser
- Large and small sticks of chalk
- Child-safe scissors
- Clay and/or playdough
- Dressing dolls with buttons, snaps, and zippers
- Easel
- Finger puppets
- Glue sticks and school glue
- Individual-size, dry-erase boards and washable, dry-erase markers
- Household items to be used with glue (such as cotton balls, cotton swabs, sponges, pieces of thread, yarn or string, pieces of fabric, pie tins or paper towel rolls)
- Lacing cards/boards and laces
- Laminated paper for pre-writing and/or letter tracing
- Materials to paint, draw, and write on (construction paper, newsprint, white paper, bubble wrap, foil, wrapping paper, and so on)
- Materials for stringing (large and small beads, string, yarn, shoelaces, and thin rope).
- Nuts, bolts, and screws of various sizes.
- Pegboards and pegs
- Puzzles (some with knobs)
- Rubber stamps and stamp pads
- Stickers
- Tongs of various sizes

(continued on the next page)

- Tools for painting (large and very small paintbrushes, cotton balls, feathers, turkey basters, paint rollers, and sponges)
- Writing utensils, such as large and small crayons, pencils (adult-size and golf-size), chalk, (large and small) and washable markers (thin and fat)

    Safety Note: Always supervise young children when using all materials on this list.

Chapter 3
I'm Three! Look What My Hands Can Do!

Your three-year-old child is growing and developing new skills every day! You can use this time of incredible change to nurture your child's fine motor skills and give her the foundation she needs to eventually learn how to hold a pencil, tie her shoes, and write her name. At three, your child is ready for activities that build strength in her upper body, refine her grasp, and help her learn how to use two hands together (bilateral hand skills).

At age three, your child may be interested in learning how to:

- Copy a circle
- Copy an accurate cross
- Thread large beads
- Build a tower of 10 1" blocks
- Tear paper
- Cut on a straight line
- Build a train with blocks (one block on top and long line behind)
- Copy a square
- Draw and paint with a variety of large tools like paintbrushes and markers)
- Put together simple, three- to four-piece puzzles
- Use glue (with supervision)
- Unbutton large buttons
- Unzip zippers
- Feed herself using a spoon and fork
- Undress and dress with some assistance

Have fun doing the activities on the following pages with your child. They will help her begin to feel confident in her ability to use her hands and will prepare her to try new skills as she gets older.

Marble Painting

Develops your child's ability to use two hands together (bilateral hand skills) and improves his eye-hand coordination.

What You Need

round, 9" pan or small box without lid | marble | paper | paint | spoon

What to Do

- Cut paper to line the bottom of the pan.
- Show your child how to dip a marble into paint with a spoon and then place the marble inside the pan.
- Have him hold the pan with two hands and maneuver it so the marble rolls the paint onto the paper in an interesting pattern.

More Fun!

- Experiment with different-sized marbles and different types of paper.
- See if he can maneuver the pan so that the painted marble leaves a big circle on the paper.

Moving Bubbles

Develops your child's ability to use two hands together (bilateral hand skills) and helps her learn how to pour liquids.

What You Need

clear, plastic lid of pie shell | measuring cup or cup for pouring water | oil | food coloring

What to Do

- Give your child a clear, plastic pie-shell lid, and help her use the measuring cup to pour equal parts of water and oil into the plastic lid. The two liquids should just cover the bottom of the lid.
- Let her choose some food coloring and help her drip four or five drops of the food coloring around the plastic lid.
- Show her how to hold the edges of the plate carefully with both hands and move it slowly from side to side.
- Observe how the colorful bubbles move around the plate.

I'm Three! Look What My Hands Can Do!

23

Toy Workshop

Increases your child's hand strength and develops your child's ability to use two hands together (bilateral hand skills)

What You Need

toy hammers, screwdrivers, and mallets | large nuts and bolts that fit together | small pieces of PVC pipe and connectors | heavy-duty plastic or wooden toys | broken toys

What to Do

- As you play with your child, show him how to use the tools and how to put various materials like nuts and bolts together.
- Have fun building new toys or "repairing" broken toys.

More Fun!

- Add an empty toolbox to give your child more opportunities to sort tools and materials.

Floor Drawing

Develops the foundations for your child's fine motor skills and increases her upper-body strength

What You Need

large sheets of paper | tape (recommended) | cardboard or other hard surface to write on (if doing the activity on carpet) | large markers, crayons, and/or paintbrushes

What to Do

- Clear some space so your child can spread out on the floor. If you are using a carpeted area, make sure you have a length of cardboard or some other hard material that she can use for a drawing surface.
- If you can, tape the paper to the floor or cardboard.
- Give her markers, crayons, and other drawing tools, and invite her to lie down on her stomach to create her masterpiece. Offer small pillows or blankets for her to put under her elbows to keep her comfortable on the hard floor.

More Fun!

- Try this activity outdoors to inspire your child to draw pictures of nature.

I'm Three! Look What My Hands Can Do!

25

Styrofoam Construction

Develops your child's finger strength

What You Need

pieces of Styrofoam | duct or packing tape | golf tees | toy hammers or small mallets

What to Do

- To control a potentially messy situation, cover the outside edges of the Styrofoam with tape.
- Encourage your child to use the hammers and mallets to build something with the Styrofoam and golf tees.
- Demonstrate how he can push golf tees into the Styrofoam with his fingers and with the hammer.
  Safety Note: Always observe closely to ensure your child uses the hammer and golf tees safely.

More Fun!

- Give your child large markers so he can decorate his building.
- Ask him to see how tall he can build his Styrofoam building.

Corn Picking

Enhances your child's pincer grasp and improves her eye-hand coordination

What You Need

Indian corn | large plastic container | sand toys, such as small buckets and shovels, plastic spoons, and large funnels

What to Do

- Put the Indian corn in a plastic container and show your child how to "pick" the corn kernels off the ears.
- After she removes all of the corn kernels, she can have fun using the sand toys and her fingers to scoop and pour the kernels.
- Encourage her to try to pick up individual kernels, which will help her improve her pincer grasp—an important pre-writing skill.

More Fun!

- Add small plastic bottles, such as medicine bottles or travel-size bottles, to the bucket. Show your child how to fill the bottles with kernels, put on the lids, and use them as shakers.

I'm Three! Look What My Hands Can Do!

27

Squeezy Water Play

Improves your child's grasp strength

What You Need

turkey basters and eyedroppers | sponges in a variety of sizes, such as makeup sponges, kitchen sponges, natural sponges, or large cleaning sponges | large plastic container with water | plastic cups and bottles

What to Do

● Show your child how to fill turkey basters, eyedroppers, and sponges with water. Encourage him to fill up cups or bottles, dump out the water, and fill them up again.

More Fun!

● Add liquid soap to the water to add a new dimension to the activity.
● To really focus on his pincer grasp, cut the sponges into small 1″–2″ pieces.

Stamp Art

Improves your child's grasp and increases finger strength

What You Need

paper | variety of stamps with small handles | washable inkpads | large washable markers

What to Do

- Give your child paper, stamps, and inkpads and show her how to use them.
- When she is interested, show her how to use a marker to color the stamp rather than using the inkpad.
- Encourage her to explore different methods of using stamps to make art.
- Talk with your child about her creations.

More Fun!

- Make soap stamps by cutting small pieces of soap in half and carving out shapes or designs (adult only). Ink will adhere to most soap, but Ivory® soap works well.

I'm Three! Look What My Hands Can Do!

29

Vertical Board Play

Refines your child's grasp and helps develop his proper forearm posture and wrist positioning

What You Need

felt board and small felt pieces | magnetic board and small magnetic pieces such as shapes, animals, or letters | easel with tray or wall

What to Do

- Place the magnetic board or felt board in a vertical position by putting it on an easel or propping it securely against a wall.
- Encourage your child to play with the magnetic pieces on the vertical board. Ask him to make up a story with the animals or build a tower out of the different shapes. This will help him develop appropriate forearm and wrist positioning and grasp.

More Fun!

- Read a story and ask your child to pick appropriate pieces and use them to re-enact the story on the vertical board.

Mini-Muffin Sorting

Improves your child's grasp of small objects and strengthens her eye-hand coordination

What You Need

mini-muffin pans | small items to sort, such as buttons, tiny pegs, stones, marbles, coins, or paper clips

What to Do

- Set out the various small items and challenge your child to sort the items into matching groups and place each group into a different mini-muffin cup (for example, putting all marbles together).

More Fun!

- Sort the objects using other criteria, such as color, shape, or weight.
- Help your child count the number of objects inside one muffin hole.

I'm Three! Look What My Hands Can Do!

31

Hide and Seek Playdough

Develops your child's hand strength and improves finger coordination

What You Need

playdough | small objects, such as marbles, coins, pegs, or animals

What to Do

- Set out the playdough and small objects to explore.
- Hide a few of the objects inside some of the playdough, and invite your child to find them.

More Fun!

- Place small cups at the table. Ask your child to place each object she finds inside the playdough into a small cup. Then help her count how many objects she found.
- Invite her to close her eyes and try to find the objects hidden in the playdough using only her fingers.
- Cutting playdough improves hand strength, so give your child scissors and encourage her to cut the playdough into pieces.

Sand Castle Clay

Improves your child's hand strength and enhances her fine motor coordination

What You Need

large bowl and a spoon for mixing (Note: Sand may scratch the bowl during mixing.) | 1 cup sand | 1 package Jell-O® sugar-free gelatin | $\frac{1}{2}$ cup cornstarch | $\frac{3}{4}$ cup hot water | 1 tsp alum (found in the spice aisle of your grocery store) | food coloring

Note: Double the recipe if you want to do the activity below in More Fun!

What to Do

- Mix all the ingredients together in a large bowl (adult-only step).
- Allow the clay to cool (adult-only step), and then knead it.
- Encourage your child to mold sand castles with her hands.
- Observe how your child uses her hands to manipulate the clay.

More Fun!

- Provide sand tools, such as small hand-held shovels, buckets, or craft sticks, and small shells for decorating castles.

I'm Three! Look What My Hands Can Do!

33

"Pop" Straws

Develops your child's pre-scissor skills

What You Need

plastic straws (must be thick plastic) | child-safe scissors

What to Do

- Show your child how to hold a straw with one hand and snip pieces from it with the scissors. Say "Pop!" as he cuts the straw.
- Encourage him to cut his straw and listen for the "pop!"

More Fun!

- Provide paper and glue for him to use to make unusual artwork with his pieces of straw.
- Help him stack or build "structures" with straw pieces and glue.

Card Cutting

Helps your child practice holding scissors appropriately

What You Need

card-weight paper including magazine inserts, junk mailings, greeting cards, or index cards | child-safe scissors

What to Do

- Cut greeting cards into single pieces (instead of folded), so they are easier for your child to manipulate.
- Show her the proper way to hold and cut with scissors. Give her verbal cues, such as "Thumb on top!" or "Open, close, open, close."
- Invite her to cut the cards with scissors, and help her hold the scissors correctly, if necessary.

More Fun!

- Make a shaker out of scrap card pieces. Help your child cut her card into pieces of confetti. Place the confetti inside a clean, clear, dry plastic bottle. Secure the lid onto the bottle with glue.

I'm Three! Look What My Hands Can Do!

35

Clothespin Airplanes

Develops your child's pre-scissor skills and hand strength

What You Need

wooden clothespins (squeeze type) | craft sticks | glue (wood glue works best) | pizza boards or pieces of cardboard

What to Do

- Help your child glue a craft stick to one stem of the squeezable end of a clothespin. The craft stick should be perpendicular to the clothespin, similar to a tail wing for an airplane. Allow to dry thoroughly.
- Give him a piece of cardboard to use as a runway and show him how to squeeze the clothespins with his fingers on the "tail wing" so that the airplane will open.
- He can take the plane in for a landing by placing clothespins around the edges of the cardboard.

More Fun!

- Encourage him to use markers, paint, or glitter to decorate his airplanes or design his runways.
- Hang runways vertically at his shoulder height to add a new landing challenge.

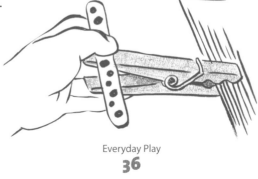

Shredded Paper Collage

Develops your child's eye-hand coordination and the
ability to use two hands to tear paper

What You Need

pieces of medium-weight paper, such as construction paper or paper bags

pieces of light-weight paper, such as newspaper or magazines | glue sticks or

small bowls of glue | paper (for the collage base)

What to Do

- Encourage your child to use two hands to tear strips of paper to make shredded paper.
- Encourage her to glue the shredded paper onto a clean piece of paper to make a collage. She may use glue sticks or dip the strips of paper into glue.
- Talk about her creation. Is the collage flat or raised? Are the shredded pieces of paper long or short?

More Fun!

- Invite her to paint her shredded paper collage after the glue dries. This will add another dimension to the art.
- Sprinkle glitter on the collage while the glue is still wet.

I'm Three! Look What My Hands Can Do!

37

Squirt Game

*Develops your child's hand strength for scissor skills
and his eye-hand coordination*

What You Need

small, plastic spray bottles filled with water | bath soap foam (color foam
works best) | finger paint paper or wax paper | plastic shower curtain
or sheet | easel or wall

What to Do

Note: This is a great outdoor activity.

- Cover the floor with a shower curtain or
  sheet and clip or tape paper to an easel
  or the wall.
- Help your child make a target by squirting
  bath-soap foam in a circle (target shape)
  on the paper. Ask your child to squirt
  the target with water.
- See how many squirts it takes to
  wash the target away.

More Fun!

- Experiment with different sizes and
  distances for the target.

Tong Pick-Up

Helps your child practice opening and closing tools and builds hand strength and coordination

What You Need

variety of tongs (large, small, plastic, metal) | variety of tweezers (large, small, plastic, metal) | small objects, such as cotton balls, cotton swabs, pieces of sponge, crayons, small blocks, pegs, or Lego blocks | variety of containers

What to Do

- Show your child how to use tongs and tweezers to pick up small objects.
- Encourage her to use the tongs and tweezers to place objects into the various containers.
- Ask her which objects are easier and which objects are more difficult to pick up with the tools. Why?

More Fun!

- Add playdough to the activity. Your child can roll small balls and snakes, or she can tear the playdough into pieces to pick up with tongs or tweezers.
- See how many objects she can put into a container without dropping one.

I'm Three! Look What My Hands Can Do!

39

Body Shapes

Improves your child's bilateral coordination, helps him identify shapes, and develops his pre-writing skills

What You Need

No materials needed

What to Do

- Show your child an example of a line (for example: vertical, horizontal, or diagonal) or shape (for example: circle, square, or triangle).
- Ask him to use his body to form that line or shape.
- If he is having difficulty, demonstrate how to make the line or shape with your body.
- Talk with your child about the characteristics of the shape. For instance, a circle is round and a square has four sides.
- Encourage your child to try to make the shape again, and help him as needed.

More Fun!

- Take photographs of your child making the Body Shapes. Hang the photos alongside a drawing of the corresponding shape so he has a model to look at later when he is trying to make the shape again.

Cardboard Stencils

Helps your child learn how to draw shapes and develops the foundations for writing

What You Need

scrap pieces of cardboard (two-ply cardboard works well) | adult scissors or knife (for adult use only) | large markers or large crayons | paper and card stock

What to Do

- Cut out circles, squares, and triangles from cardboard (adult-only step). **Note:** Shapes that are 4"–6" in diameter work best for preschool-aged children. Save the outside pieces of cardboard to use as stencils.

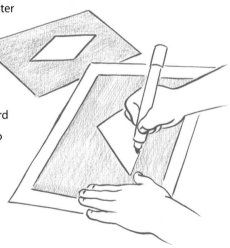

- Show your child how to use cardboard shapes and stencils. Encourage her to use one hand to hold the stencil and the other hand to trace around the edge.

More Fun!

- To encourage a good grasp and wrist posture, use clips to place stencils on easels. This will give your child the experience of writing on a vertical surface.
- Invite her to use the card stock to create greeting cards and to decorate them with the stencils.

I'm Three! Look What My Hands Can Do!

41

No-Mess Fingerpainting

Develops your child's finger isolation and helps him learn to make simple lines or shapes

What You Need

resealable plastic freezer bags | fingerpaints

What to Do

- Give your child a resealable plastic freezer bag.
- After he chooses the color that he wants, help him pour the fingerpaint into his bag.
- Help him close and seal the bag securely. Make sure the bag does not have excess air inside.
- Place the sealed bag flat on the table or floor and show your child how to use his index fingers to make lines or shapes in the paint.
- Talk about the different shapes or designs that your child makes.

More Fun!

- Squirt two different colors of paint into the bag. Encourage your child to use his index finger to mix the paint together.
- Explore the new colors he creates by mixing paint.

Racing Tracks

Develops your child's foundations for writing

What You Need

large sheet of paper | paint, markers, or electrical tape | variety of small cars and trucks

What to Do

- Cut a sheet of paper large enough to cover your entire tabletop or floor space.
- Help your child draw or use electrical tape to make a racetrack, using circles and large vertical, horizontal, and diagonal lines.
  Note: Keep the pattern simple and make lines a solid color.
- Encourage your child to drive her cars and trucks on the racetrack.
- Ask her to identify the round and straight lines of the track.

More Fun!

- Help your child design and draw her own tracks by using a variety of lines and shapes.
- Encourage her to dip the wheels of the cars into paint and then trace the lines and shapes of the tracks.

Wall Washing

Develops your child's pre-writing skills

What You Need

large adult-size paintbrushes (at least 3" wide) or paint rollers | large bucket of water | liquid soap (if you want to use soapy water) | sidewalk chalk | outside wall or fence

What to Do

- Encourage your child to use sidewalk chalk to draw large circles, crosses, and horizontal, vertical, and diagonal lines on the outside wall or fence.
- Give him a bucket of water and paintbrushes or rollers and invite him to "wash the wall" with the paintbrushes or rollers.
- Show him how to trace the lines or shapes with the wet paintbrush to make the drawing disappear.

More Fun!

- Use large sponges or rags instead of paintbrushes to wash the wall.

Yarn Shapes

Develops your child's ability to trace simple shapes and to use glue and other art materials in play

What You Need

paper with horizontal lines, vertical lines, circles, squares, and triangles drawn on it | markers | glue stick or cotton swabs and small bowl of glue | yarn pre-cut into various lengths

What to Do

- Give your child the paper with lines or shapes drawn on it and encourage her to trace over the lines or shapes with glue.
- Glue yarn to the lines or shapes.
- Talk about the shapes she made.
- Once the glue is dry, she can feel and trace the yarn shapes with her fingers.

More Fun!

- Give her a blank sheet of paper and invite her to make her own yarn lines or shapes.
- Use the completed yarn shapes as templates and trace inside or outside the shapes with markers.
- You can also use the completed sheet with the yarn shapes to make a simple crayon rubbing. Place a sheet of plain paper on top and rub back and forth with a crayon. See what happens!

I'm Three! Look What My Hands Can Do!

45

Cup Tower

Gives your child experience with lacing and develops
his eye-hand coordination

What You Need

small paper cups, such as bathroom cups | coffee stirrers or
plastic straws | pieces of Styrofoam | markers,
crayons, stickers, and other materials

What to Do

- Poke a small hole in the bottom of each small
  paper drinking cup (adult-only step). Make sure
  the hole is just big enough for the straw or
  coffee stirrer.
- Encourage your child to use coffee stirrers or
  plastic straws to string the paper cups together.
- Show him how to stick one end of the straw
  into a Styrofoam base, to make the cup tower stand tall.
- Talk about how many cups can fit on one straw. Ask your child questions. For
  instance, "How tall is the finished tower?"

More Fun!

- If your child has difficulty holding or lacing the cups, consider having him
  place one end of the straw into the Styrofoam before beginning. This will
  hold the straw steady.
- Decorate the paper cups with markers, crayons, and stickers.

Ribbon Pull

Improves your child's pincer grasp

What You Need

clean coffee can with plastic lid | variety of ribbon | scissors and sharp knife (for use by adults only)

What to Do

- Cut pieces of ribbon into different lengths at least 12" long (adult-only step).
- Use a knife to cut slits in the coffee can lid for each ribbon; thread ribbons through the slits (adult-only step).
- Tie a knot on one end of each ribbon. (The knot should be inside the can when you secure the lid.)
- Position the ribbons so that a small piece of each one sticks out from the top of the lid.
- Secure the lid (adult-only step).
- Show your child how to pull each ribbon with her fingers.
- Invite her to pull the ribbons out of the can. Once all the ribbons are as far out of the can as possible, remove the lid and reposition the ribbons to start again.

More Fun!

- Before beginning, ask your child to predict which ribbon will be the longest. Once all the ribbons are out, talk about the colors, textures, lengths, and widths. Help her determine which ribbon is the longest and which is the shortest.

I'm Three! Look What My Hands Can Do!

Shish-Kabob Snack

Develops your child's bilateral hand skills and expands his eye-hand coordination

What You Need

foods that are easy to skewer, such as bananas, pineapple, strawberries, melon, or marshmallows | wooden shish-kabob skewers or chopsticks

What to Do

- Give your child a wooden skewer or chopstick.
  Safety Note: Skewers have sharp ends, so be sure to supervise this activity.
- Let him choose the foods and show him how to lace the food onto the skewer.
- Talk about the shapes and colors of food items.
- After he finishes making his shish-kabob snack, he can eat and enjoy it!

More Fun!

- Challenge him to see how many pieces of food will fit on a skewer.
- Suggest that he create a food pattern, such as banana, pineapple, banana, pineapple.

Straw Jewelry

Develops your child's eye-hand coordination and improves bilateral hand skills

What You Need

colorful straws | child-safe scissors | plastic string for making jewelry

What to Do

- Invite your child to cut straws into small pieces, $\frac{1}{2}$"–1" in length.

  Note: See "Pop" Straws activity on page 34 for more ideas with straws.
- Help her cut a piece of string long enough for a necklace or bracelet.
- Tie a large knot in one end of string.
- Encourage your child to string pieces of straw onto the string.
- When the string is full of straw pieces, help your child tie the two ends together to make a bracelet or necklace.

More Fun!

- See if your child can make a pattern by using different colors of straw pieces. Simple patterns using two colors will work well for three-year-olds.

I'm Three! Look What My Hands Can Do!

49

Walk Like an Animal

Develops your child's upper-body strength and improves bilateral coordination

What You Need

No materials needed

What to Do

- This is a great activity to try inside or outside although it requires a certain amount of open floor space.
- Sing the song "This is the way we walk like a (insert animal name)" to the tune of "Here We Go 'Round the Mulberry Bush."
- Select animals that your child can imitate. Animals that require him to place his hands or his body on the floor will build more strength in the upper body. Some suggestions include: bear, cat, dog, snake, frog, crab, and giraffe.
- Demonstrate how to "walk" like the animal.
- Encourage him to move his body and pretend to be each animal.

Chapter 4
Now I'm Four So I Can Do More!

At age four, many children expand their repertoire of fine motor skills dramatically. Your child may learn to use thin writing and drawing utensils to trace, copy, and form a variety of shapes. He may also gain independence in simple scissor skills, such as cutting on a straight line. At this age, your child may enjoy manipulating clay, playdough, and sand and exploring new tools to create artwork. These experiences are necessary to prepare his hands for more challenging fine motor activities.

At age four, your child may be interested in learning how to:

- Cut out large shapes (for example: circle, square, triangle)
- Copy a square
- Copy a triangle
- Copy a cross
- Draw a person (may include a circle with two lines or be as detailed as a head, body, legs, arms and fingers)
- Make marks to represent her name
- Draw and paint with a variety of sizes and types of utensils (such as markers, paintbrushes, pencils, or crayons)
- Put together simple puzzles
- String small beads
- Use an easy-to-squeeze 1-hole punch and stapler, with close supervision
- Lace simple cards
- Manipulate clay or playdough with his hands

- Use tools such as a play hammer, rolling pin, or plastic knife with clay or playdough
- Use fingers to act out simple fingerplays and songs
- Use a zipper independently (may need help starting)
- Button large buttons
- Snap easy snaps
- Pour liquid into a cup
- Draw a picture that does not include all the characteristics of objects known to her (for instance, she may draw a square for a car and leave out the wheels)
- Attempt to sign her name (although she may often delete, reverse, inaccurately form letters, or write them from right to left)
- Undress and dress independently

Your child may hold a crayon with his thumb, index, and middle fingers in a more basic way, with his ring and pinky fingers slightly bent and held high up on the pencil; or he may hold it with the tips of his thumb, index, and middle fingers, ring and pinky fingers bent, moving his hand separately from his forearm.

Have fun doing the activities on the following pages with your child. They are designed with four-year-old children in mind, and they address more challenging precursors of fine motor skills, such as refined grasp of utensils and coordinating two hands together. They will prepare your child for the fine motor tasks she'll need in kindergarten.

Crayon Rubbings

Improves your child's eye-hand coordination

What You Need

large and/or small crayons with paper peeled off | white drawing paper | flat objects with texture, such as leaves and coins | templates of shapes, letters, or animals

What to Do

- Ask your child to select an object.
- Ask him to close his eyes and feel the object with his fingers.
- Show him how to place the paper on top of the object and color over it.
- Talk about his creations and label them by the objects he used to make them.

More Fun!

- Give your child black paper and chalk to create more rubbings.
- Choose new or unusual objects to use in crayon rubbings.
- Encourage his imagination (for example, ask him, "What if the object isn't flat?" "What if the object doesn't have a texture?").

Dressing Up

Gives your child practice with using zippers and manipulating buttons and snaps, and encourages her independence in dressing

What You Need

dress-up clothes with zippers | dress-up clothes with large buttons | dress-up clothes with simple snaps

What to Do

- Give your child dress-up clothing that includes zippers, large buttons, and snaps, and show her how to use them, if necessary.
- If your child can't do it independently, start the process and allow her to finish. For example, help her place the button inside the buttonhole and then help her pull the button through. This technique will help your child develop confidence in her attempts at fastening.

More Fun!

- Use dolls or stuffed animals with fasteners on their clothing to give her another opportunity to develop independence in dressing.

Finger Puppets

Develops your child's finger coordination

What You Need

child-size gloves (small women's gloves may also work) | scissors (adult-use only) | school glue or fabric glue in small bowls and cotton swabs (school glue will require more drying time) | markers | sequins, small buttons, small pom-poms, and plastic eyes

What to Do

- Cut the fingers out of the gloves (adult-only step).
- Give your child at least two finger puppets to decorate with markers, sequins, buttons, small pom-poms, and plastic eyes.
- After the glue dries, invite him to use his finger puppets to put on a show.
- Encourage him to use puppets on both hands in his finger puppet show.

More Fun!

- Ask him to act out a favorite story, book, or song with his finger puppets.

Photo Puzzles

Gives your child practice with putting together simple puzzles and using various tools in play

What You Need

digital camera | printer | thick paper, such as card stock or oak tag | glue sticks | child-size scissors | resealable plastic bags to store puzzles after use

What to Do

- Use the digital camera to take a close-up photograph of your child.
- Print the photograph on 5" x 7" or 8" x 10" photo paper.
- Give your child a piece of card stock to fit her photograph (5" x 7" or 8" x 10"), and have her glue the photograph to the card stock. Allow it to dry completely.
- Show her how to cut the attached photographs into six or eight irregularly shaped puzzle pieces, and help her, as needed.
- Encourage her to take apart and put together her own puzzle.

More Fun!

- If a camera and printer are not available, use magazine photos instead.
- Make puzzles out of photographs of her favorite people or pets.

Cookie Decorating

Refines your child's grasp and release and builds hand strength

What You Need

sugar cookies | cake icing | edible sprinkles | tubes of decorating icing (squeeze type) | plastic knives and spoons

What to Do

- Encourage your child to spread icing onto cookies using knives or spoons.
- Encourage him to use his fingers to place sprinkles—one pinch at a time—on his cookies. Eat and enjoy!

More Fun!

- Offer toothpicks for him to draw designs in the icing.

Drops of Color

Develops your child's grasp and pre-scissor skills

What You Need

medicine droppers | food coloring | water | small bowl(s) | coffee filters
(basket-style work best)

What to Do

- Mix food coloring with water in a bowl. You may prefer to use several colors in different bowls for this activity.
- Show your child how to fill the medicine dropper with colored water. Then, show her how to squeeze the medicine dropper to make "drops of color" on the coffee filter.
- Let her create her own "drops of color" on the filters.

More Fun!

- The "drops of color" art makes a very interesting sun catcher. Help your child punch a hole in the top of the filter and tie on a piece of string. Hang the art in front of a window. Laminate if desired.

Reusable Stickers

Improves your child's grasp and release of small objects

What You Need

reusable stickers, such as Colorforms, Unisets, or window stickers | small dry-erase board or unbreakable hand-held mirror | easel or incline board (see Incline Writing Boards activity on page 71 for instructions)

What to Do

- Place a dry-erase board or mirror on an easel or incline board.
- Encourage your child to use stickers to decorate the board or tell a story.
- When the play is over, ask him to remove stickers and replace them into storage.

More Fun!

- Provide dry-erase markers for your child to trace around re-usable stickers.
- If possible, let him decorate a nearby window with stickers.

Seed Art

Helps your child develop her pincer grasp

What You Need

variety of seeds, such as pumpkin, sunflower, or apple | glue | small bowls or nut cups | cotton swabs | construction paper | large markers | shape templates

What to Do

- Encourage your child to draw shapes on her construction paper. Alternately, she may use templates to trace shapes.
  Note: Do not cut out the shapes.
- Pour glue into small bowls, provide cotton swabs for dipping, and pour seeds into small bowls or nut cups (adult-only step). Use a separate bowl for each type of seed.
- Show your child how to use the cotton swabs to dab glue onto her shapes, and invite her to place seeds onto the glued area, remaining inside the traced area.
- Hang the work once it dries.

Stick Houses

Gives your child practice with his pincer grasp and develops bilateral coordination

What You Need

toothpicks | glue in small container for dipping | cotton swabs | thick paper, such as index cards, oak tag, or poster board

What to Do

- Give your child a piece of thick paper to use as the "foundation" for his construction.
- Demonstrate how to dip toothpicks into glue or use cotton swabs to place glue on a structure to hold it in place.
- Encourage him to build houses with toothpicks.

More Fun!

- Read or tell the story of the "Three Little Pigs," and then encourage your child to try building with pieces of straw or craft sticks.

Tape It Up!

Develops your child's grasp strength

What You Need

masking tape | clear tape | variety of paper | child-safe scissors | paper towel rolls

What to Do

- Place the different tapes and variety of papers on a table.
- Encourage your child to tape the paper to the paper towel roll to create original work.
- Show her how to tear the tape.
- Observe how she uses the materials for self-expression.

More Fun!

- Ask your child to describe her creation and transcribe her words, if she is interested. Display the description alongside her original work.

All-Terrain Vehicles

Improves your child's hand strength

What You Need

large plastic container | various "terrains," including sand, potting soil, pebbles, pea gravel, and mulch | variety of very small toy trucks or construction vehicles

What to Do

- Prepare one "terrain" on each part of the container (For example, put sand at one end of the table and potting soil on the other end).
- Invite your child to drive his "All Terrain Vehicles" through/over the terrain.
- Ask him to build hills or mountains out of the material laid out on the table.
- Suggest that he drive his vehicles "over," "around," and "through" the hills. Demonstrate these directions, as needed.

More Fun!

- Ask your child to use his vehicles to make different track shapes in the terrain.

More Peas Please

Develops your child's grasp and improves finger strength

What You Need

green playdough | plastic bowl and spoon

What to Do

- Demonstrate how to use your thumb, index, and middle fingers to create "peas" by rolling playdough into small balls.
- Remind your child that the "peas" are pretend and are not for eating.
- Encourage her to make tiny "peas" out of the playdough.
- Once your child masters the rolling motion, challenge her to use the spoon to fill a bowl with "peas."

More Fun!

- Add plastic forks to the activity. See if your child can catch the "peas" on her fork.
- Encourage your child to use her index fingers to "smoosh" the peas.

Disappearing Holes

Gives your child experience using scissors and improves his eye-hand coordination

What You Need

polka-dot shapes (see Polka-Dot Shapes activity on page 84) |
child-safe scissors

What to Do

- Do the Polka-Dot Shapes activity on page 84 . After this, your child will have a sheet of paper with holes forming a shape (circle, square, triangle).
- Show him how to use scissors to cut out the shape by cutting through the centers of the punched holes. The cut-out shapes will have scalloped edges when he finishes cutting through the holes along the edges.
- Encourage him to stay on the polka dots as he cuts out the shapes.
- Invite him to feel and explore the edges of these new shapes.
- If your child isn't developmentally ready to cut out more elaborate shapes, use the hole punch to form simple lines (horizontal, vertical, or diagonal) for him to cut.

Making a Wreath

Develops your child's scissor skills and bilateral hand skills

What You Need

paper plates | glue sticks or small container of glue for dipping |
tissue paper | child-safe scissors

What to Do

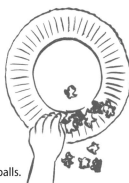

- Show your child how to fold a paper plate in half.
- Encourage her to cut a semi-circle around the inside of the paper plate.
- Unfold the plate to reveal a "wreath."
- Help your child decorate the wreath by tearing small pieces of tissue paper and squeezing the paper into balls.
- Give her a glue stick to use to cover the "wreath" in glue, or dip each tissue paper ball into glue.

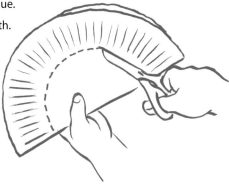

- Glue the tissue balls onto the wreath. When the glue dries, display the wreath prominently.
- Help your child punch two holes at the top of the wreath and lace yarn or ribbon through the holes so that she can hang the wreath.

More Fun!

- Use the wreath as a frame for a picture—either something your child has created or for a photo. Give it as a gift!

Paper Chains

Gives your child experience using scissors

What You Need

construction paper | child-safe scissors | glue sticks

What to Do

- Show your child how to cut strips of paper. Draw lines on the paper for your child to follow, if needed.
- Ask him to cut strips of construction paper.
- Show him how to glue the ends of the paper to form circles, and then how to link the circles together to make paper chains.

More Fun!

- Use the paper chains as decorations during holidays, for special occasions, or as measuring tools. For instance, he can measure his height with the chains.
- Cut different lengths of paper so the circles are different sizes.
- Use other kinds of paper, such as magazine pages, wrapping paper, and so on.

Place Mats

Helps your child become more adept at using scissors

What You Need

construction paper or large, plain paper bags cut into rectangles | variety of writing utensils, such as crayons, markers, paint, and glitter glue | laminating materials or clear contact paper | child-safe scissors

What to Do

- Encourage your child to decorate her construction paper or cardboard place mat in whatever way she wishes.
- Laminate it (adult-only step).
- Demonstrate how to snip the edges of the paper to make a fringe.
- Encourage your child to use child-safe scissors to create a fringe around the outside edge of the paper.

More Fun!

- Invite your child to trace around a fork, spoon, and knife in their appropriate positions on the place mat. Then she can use the place mat to help her remember how to set her place at the table.
- Laminated place mats make great gifts.

Feely Shapes

Helps your child learn to draw shapes and use his hands to manipulate small objects

What You Need

variety of fabric, such as velvet, faux fur, corduroy, denim, silk, and lace | adult scissors | cardboard, paper, and glue | writing and drawing tools

What to Do

- Cut pieces of cardboard into different shapes of various sizes from 2" across and larger. Cut matching shapes out of fabric of different textures (adult-only step). Glue the fabric to each shape and let the shapes dry.
- Encourage your child to explore the different textures of the shapes.
- Talk about the shapes and show him how to trace around them.
- Place the "Feely Shapes" inside a bag or box. Ask your child to reach into the back and identify each shape by the way it feels. Ask questions to guide him, such as, "Does it have sides? Is it round?"

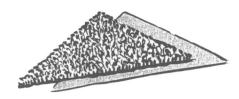

Glue Shapes and Letters

Gives your child practice in tracing shapes or letters and develops hand strength

What You Need

color glue and/or glitter glue | paper

What to Do

- Draw shapes or write your child's name on paper.
- Demonstrate how to squeeze bottles to trace the shapes or letters with glue, leaving a raised line on the paper.
- Help your child with tracing, as needed.
- Allow time to let the glue dry thoroughly.
- Encourage her to use her index finger to trace the shapes or letters of her name.

More Fun!

- Use glue shapes or letters for crayon rubbings. Place white paper on top of the glue shapes and invite your child to color over them with a crayon.

Incline Writing Boards

Develops your child's effective grasp of a writing utensil

What You Need

three-ring binder (3" size) | non-skid plastic drawer liner | large paper clips | variety of writing utensils, such as large washable markers | plain paper

What to Do

- Cut a piece of non-skid drawer liner to the size of the three-ring binder (adult-only step).
- Place the three-ring binder on top of the drawer liner, with the wide side of the binder facing away from your child. Tilt the binder slightly to the left if your child is right-handed or slightly to the right if he is left-handed.
- Help him clip paper to the incline board using a large paper clip or clothespin on the side.
- He can enjoy drawing or writing on this inclined surface.

Journal Drawing

Helps your child gain control of a writing tool and expands her pre-writing skills

What You Need

unlined paper (Young children should not write on lined paper until they are developmentally ready. See page 123) | variety of drawing tools, such as adult-size pencils, washable markers, or crayons

What to Do

- Explain to your child that journaling is a way to tell a story.
- Encourage your child to participate in "journal drawing" by asking her to draw about a particular subject or theme. For example, if you are talking about places where people live, ask her to draw a picture of the place (or places) where she lives.
- Ask her to describe her "journal drawing" to you. Transcribe her words onto the paper and read the dictation back to her. Journals can be wonderful keepsakes from your child's early years.

Mirror, Mirror, on the Wall

Develops your child's ability to draw or write on a vertical surface

What You Need

wall mirror or large, stable mirror | dry-erase markers | eraser or dry cloth

What to Do

- Have your child stand facing the mirror.
- Encourage him to use dry-erase markers to decorate himself on the mirror.
- Ideas: add hair, a mustache, a beard, a hair bow, earrings, clothes, glasses, a hat, and so on.
- When your child finishes his drawing, show him how to use the eraser to clean off the mirror.

More Fun!

- If you have a full-length mirror, help your child trace around his entire body using a dry-erase marker.

Ribbon Drawing

Develops your child's shoulder strength and gives her practice in forming shapes

What You Need

ribbon 1"–2" wide | small wooden dowel rods $\frac{1}{2}$"–1" in diameter and 8" –12" long | staple gun or duct tape

What to Do

- Cut the ribbon into 4' to 5' pieces. Staple or securely tape one end of the ribbon to the end of the dowel rod (adult-only step).
- Show your child how to hold the dowel and make the ribbon move through the air.
- Ask, "Can you draw a circle?" "A square?"
- Make a shape or a letter in the air using your ribbon, and see if she can guess what shape or letter it is. Then, ask her to copy you using her own ribbon.
- Or, sing the following song to the tune of "Put Your Finger on Your Nose":

Make a circle in the air,
In the air.
Make a circle in the air,
In the air.
Make a circle in the air
And shake it if you dare.
Make a circle in the air,
In the air.

Shape Person

Gives your child practice in tracing shapes and participating in a prewriting activity

What You Need

variety of shape stencils | washable markers | paper

What to Do

- Demonstrate one way to use shape stencils to draw a person. For example, show your child how to use a square for the head, a circle for the tummy, and triangles for legs and arms.
- Encourage your child to explore different ways to make a "shape person." He may trace the stencil or color inside the stencil.
- Ask him to tell you about his person. Transcribe his description of his person onto the paper. Ask him questions about his shape person, such as "What shapes did you use?"

More Fun!

- Give your child glitter glue, jewels, and scrap pieces of material for him to decorate his "shape person."
- Make more than one and create a story about them.
- Make them into puppets by cutting them out and attaching them to craft sticks. Have a puppet show.

Sidewalk Shadows

Develops drawing and tracing skills

What You Need

sidewalk chalk

What to Do

Note: This activity requires you and your child to work together.

- Find a safe sidewalk or paved area.
- Lie down on the sidewalk and tell your child to use sidewalk chalk to trace your body, making a "sidewalk shadow."
- Change places and trace your child's outline on the ground.
- Encourage her to add details to the "sidewalk shadows."

More Fun!

- Encourage your child to use chalk to write your names on the shadows.
- Bring buckets of water and paintbrushes out to the sidewalk. Your child can make the shadows disappear by painting them with water.

Simon Says

Encourages your child to learn directional terms needed for writing and improves coordination

What You Need

No materials needed

What to Do

- Teach your child the rules of "Simon Says."
- Play the part of Simon and give commands that include directional terms including up, down, under, and on top. For example:
  - Simon says, "Put your hands UP in the air."
  - Simon says, "Put your feet UNDER your chair."
  - Simon says, "Put your chin ON TOP OF your hand."

More Fun!

- Consider adding "left" and "right" terms to the game. Most four-year-olds have trouble differentiating between "left" and "right" so you should model the commands to help your child be successful. Stand with your back to your child and make the motions as you describe them. This will help him follow the directions.

Bead Jewelry

Gives your child experience with stringing items, develops her bilateral hand skills, and improves her eye-hand coordination

What You Need

variety of small beads (½" diameter or smaller) | plastic thread | non-skid plastic drawer liner cut into a place mat-sized rectangle | child-safe scissors

What to Do

- Place beads on the non-skid mat so that the beads will not roll away.
- After your child decides if she wants to make a bracelet or a necklace, give her child-safe scissors to cut the thread to the appropriate length. Help your child cut the thread, if necessary.
- Tie a knot in the end of the thread.
- She can string the beads to create a masterpiece.
- Help her tie the two ends of the thread together when she finishes stringing the beads.

More Fun!

- Challenge your child to make a repeating pattern with the beads.
- Place the beads on the non-skid mat and help her plan a pattern before stringing the beads. Talk with your child about the patterns.

Make Your Own Lacing Cards

Develops your child's eye-hand coordination and his confidence in using tools

What You Need

old greeting cards | child-safe scissors | 1-hole punch | yarn or string | duct tape

What to Do

- Set out the child-safe scissors and old greeting cards and invite your child to choose one of the cards. Show him how to cut the card along the fold, so that he ends up with two pieces that are the same size.
- Show him how to use a 1-hole punch, and ask him to punch holes around the edges of the cards.
- Measure out a length of yarn that will cover the card, with a bit left over. Cut the yarn and cover one end with a piece of duct tape to make a tip. Your child may need help with some, or all, of this step.
- Encourage him to lace the yarn through his card.

Tambourine

Develops your child's lacing skills and her ability to use various tools to create objects

What You Need

paper plates | fingerpaints, or paints and brushes | buttons | stapler |
1-hole punch | spoon | yarn and large markers or crayons

What to Do

- Give your child two paper plates and invite her to decorate the bottoms of the plates with fingerpaints or paints and brushes.
- Help your child staple the decorated paper plates together, keeping the staples around the outside, but leaving approximately 1" along the edge for hole-punching. Leave a 2" opening at the top of the plates for filling.
- Help her use a spoon to put buttons inside joined plates, and assist her in stapling closed the remaining opening at the top.
- Encourage your child to use the 1-hole punch around the outside edge of the plate (beyond the staples so that buttons cannot fall out).
- Give her a length of yarn with a large knot at one end and she can lace up the tambourine.
- Tie off the end of the yarn and trim the excess, when finished (adult-only step).
- Turn on music or sing and shake the tambourine to the beat or have a parade!

Beauty Salon and Barber Shop

Improves your child's bilateral hand skills

What You Need

large male and female dolls with hair | hairbrushes, combs, and curlers | foam soap and craft sticks for shaving | various decorative hair items such as clips, barrettes, rubber bands, and hair bows | cotton balls, cotton swabs, and makeup brushes or small paintbrushes

What to Do

- Has your child ever been to a salon or barber shop? If so, ask him if he can tell you what types of things happen there. You may expand on your child's ideas about the salon or barber shop by talking about different services that barbers and salon employees provide.
- Set out the various materials and encourage your child to use them to style his doll's hair or pretend to cut it.
- Help him learn the correct ways to use the grooming tools.

More Fun!

- Add play money to the area so the dolls can pay for his services. Your child can manipulate, count, and sort the coins and paper money.

Kite Flying

Develops your child's eye-hand coordination

What You Need

thick paper, such as oak tag, card stock, or construction paper | yarn or string | stapler, 1-hole punch, and tape

What to Do

- Show your child what a large diamond shape looks like.
- Then, ask her to draw two large diamond shapes (as close to the same size as she can) on her paper to cut out.
  Note: Many four-year-olds will draw a square or shape other than a diamond, which will work fine for this project.
- Show her how to put the matching "diamonds" together using a stapler or tape.
- Help her cut a piece of yarn or string for the kite tail and punch a hole at the bottom of the kite.
- Invite your child to thread the yarn through the hole and help her tie a knot to secure it.
- Next, help her cut another piece of string to fly the kite with. Punch a hole at the top of the kite, thread the yarn through the hole, and tie a knot.
- Encourage her to hold onto the kite string and run around to "fly" her kite inside or outside.

More Fun!

- Set out markers and other materials for her to decorate her kite.

Making a Collage

*Gives your child experience using scissors, and
experimenting with various materials*

What You Need

variety of materials to cut or tear, including construction paper, greeting cards,
junk mail, foil, tissue paper, wrapping paper, and newspaper | poster board or
oak tag cut in half- or quarter-pieces | glue sticks and school glue |
child-safe scissors

What to Do

- Talk to your child about how to make a collage.
- Set out the various materials and encourage him to choose, cut and tear, then
  glue the materials to the poster board or oak tag to make his own collage.
- Find a prominent place to display the collages that he makes.

More Fun!

- Provide collage items that do not need to be cut, such as cotton balls, small
  pom-poms, felt scraps, pieces of yarn, and ribbon.

Polka-Dot Shapes

Gives your child experience cutting with scissors and improves her grasp strength

What You Need

construction paper cut in half, 5" x 7" index cards, or 5" x 7" cardstock | marker | 1-hole punch

What to Do

- Using a marker, draw a large shape (at least 4" across) on a piece of paper. Make sure the lines of the shape are close to the edges of the paper.
- Show your child a 1-hole punch and how to use it, and then have her try it herself.
- Encourage her to punch holes along the edge of the shape.

More Fun!

- Use the hole punch to create simple lines or letters.
- Use the "polka-dot shape" as a template. Show your child how to place the "polka-dot shape" on another piece of paper and use markers to color in each hole. Lift the template to see the shape. Connect the dots to form the shape.

Chapter 5
I'm Ready for Kindergarten!

Your five-year-old is becoming more confident in her ability to use tools and materials like scissors, tape, glue, and hole-punches. As she reaches her sixth birthday, she may have established a consistent grasp pattern that she will use for holding writing utensils and for self-care tasks. During the year, she may also develop a growing interest in writing as a form of self-expression, learning how to write her name and other letters of the alphabet that are relevant to her, such as letters for the words "mom" and "dad."

At age five, your child may be interested in learning how to:

- Draw a person with facial features, limbs, and other details (proportions are unrealistic)
- Build steps with small blocks
- Imitate drawing a diamond shape
- Write his first name and a few letters (may include letter omissions and/or letter reversals—letters may not be in a straight line)
- Create symbolic representations of objects with clay or playdough (may not resemble the real objects)
- Create symbolic representations of objects through drawing or painting (may not resemble the real objects)
- Sign and label drawings (may include inventive spelling, letter omissions, and/or letter reversals)
- Lace shoes
- Use a knife to spread/apply butter, jelly, and so on
- Put together puzzles of at least six pieces
- Use scissors to cut out small shapes and various designs (approximately 1" across)

- Use scissors to cut non-paper materials such as yarn or tape
- Use tools such as glue stick, 1-hole punch, stapler, and tape, with little supervision
- Button/unbutton smaller buttons
- Snap/unsnap simple fasteners
- Use his fingers to act out fingerplays that require isolated finger movements, as in, "Where Is Thumbkin?"
- Use dynamic tripod grasp (holds tool with tips of thumb, index, and middle fingers; ring and pinky fingers bent) or quadripod grasp (holds tool with tips of thumb, index, middle, and ring fingers, with pinky bent) when using writing utensils

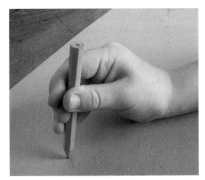 

Quadripod grasp   **Dynamic Tripod grasp**

Enjoy this year of growth with your five-year-old. Help her expand her fine motor skills by doing the activities in this chapter, and watch her skills improve even further during her kindergarten year!

Geoboards

Develops your child's finger strength, bilateral coordination, and in-hand manipulation skills

What You Need

Geoboard—can be commercially purchased or handmade (see More Fun! below) | rubber bands with good elasticity in a variety of sizes

What to Do

- Invite your child to explore the Geoboard and rubber bands.
- Demonstrate the method of stretching a rubber band from one peg to the next. Form lines, shapes, or letters with the rubber bands.
- Encourage your child to make her own lines, shapes, or letters on the Geoboard with rubber bands.

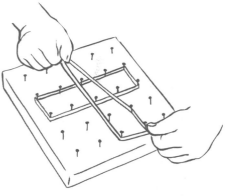

More Fun!

- Make a Geoboard. To make a Geoboard, you will need the following:

    square piece of wood (approximately 5" x 5") | sandpaper | 25 finishing nails (1") | ruler | hammer

To make your own Geoboard, go to a building supply store and ask someone to cut a square piece of wood. Sand the edges until smooth. Use a hammer to insert 25 finishing nails into the wood in an evenly spaced pattern of five rows with five nails each 1" apart. To allow room for the rubber bands, nails should extend $1/2$" out from the surface of the wood.

Graph Paper Art

Refines your child's hand movements necessary for writing, develops good eye-hand coordination, and helps him use an age-appropriate grasp of writing utensil

What You Need

Large-grid (at least $1/4$") graph paper (may be printed for free off the Internet) | colored pencils

What to Do

- Give your child a piece of graph paper and colored pencils.
- Encourage him to color in the squares to create "Graph Paper Art."

More Fun!

- Form letters by coloring in squares of the graph paper. Draw a letter on the graph paper and then see if your child can copy it.
- Give him graph paper and watercolors or tempera paint and small paintbrushes with which he can explore painting squares or other shapes and designs.

Making Tracks

Develops your child's small muscle control and improves her eye-hand coordination

What You Need

large sheets of paper | paper plates | various small toy vehicles, such as cars, trucks, vans, or construction vehicles | fingerpaint or tempera paint and markers | bowl of water | sponges or small brushes | paper towel

What to Do

- Write your child's name on a large sheet of paper. Use bubble-type letters that are large enough to serve as a track for small vehicles.
- Pour paint onto paper plates, and put some vehicles on the table.
- Encourage your child to experiment with making tracks by rolling a vehicle through the paint and then rolling the vehicle over paper.
- Show your child her "Name Track." Invite her to roll a vehicle through the paint and trace the letters of her name with the vehicle to "make tracks."
- When your child begins to lose interest in the activity, give her a bowl of water and small sponges or brushes to wash off the vehicles. Set them on a paper towel to dry.

More Fun!

- Some children may be able to make their name tracks independently, without having to follow the letter outlines.
- Provide blank sheets of paper and encourage your child to make new letter tracks on her paper.

Stick Letters

Develops your child's eye-hand coordination and helps him learn how to form letters of the alphabet

What You Need

craft sticks | scissors (adult-use only) | glue (squeezable or stick) | construction paper | washable markers

What to Do

- Cut several craft sticks crosswise into halves and fourths (adult-only step). After cutting them, sand any rough edges.
- Write capital letters on the paper so that your child has an example to copy.
- Give your child various sizes of craft sticks, and encourage him to make "stick letters" by arranging the pieces of craft sticks on the construction paper.
  Note: Letters with curves will be more challenging to make, but encourage him to try to use small pieces of craft sticks to form them.
- He can glue his letters to the construction paper, and then give them time to dry.
- Once the glue is dry, he can use markers to trace around his "stick letters" on paper or decorate the letters.

More Fun!

- Use sticks to write names or words that are interesting to your child.
- Your child may need you to write the letters on his paper so he can place the craft sticks directly on the lines.

Paper Flowers

Develops your child's scissor skills, and strengthens her eye-hand coordination

What You Need

thin, 8 ½" X 11" copying paper in various colors | child-safe scissors (sharp enough to cut thin paper) | chenille sticks

What to Do

- After your child selects the paper for her flowers, help her use the scissors to cut the paper in half to form an 8 ½ x 5 ½ rectangle.
- Demonstrate how to accordion-pleat the paper, starting on the long side of the paper. Help her as needed.
- Ask her to hold the pleated paper while you help her wind one end of a chenille stick around the center of the paper.
- She can separate layers of the paper by gently pulling the paper apart at the edges of the flower.

More Fun!

- Place the flowers into a piece of Styrofoam and then inside the "Painted Flower Pot" (see Painted Flower Pots on page 116) for a beautiful gift or decoration.

Where Is Thumbkin?

Develops your child's eye-hand coordination and his ability to move individual fingers (finger isolation)

What You Need

No materials needed

What to Do

- Sing the song "Where Is Thumbkin?" and demonstrate the related hand movements as you go.
- Show your child how to hold his fingers down to help isolate one finger for movement.

  Note: The middle and ring fingers are typically the hardest to isolate and individualize. Your child may need to hold down the other fingers until he masters this new motor pattern.

More Fun!

- "This Old Man" is another good fingerplay that gives your child the opportunity to develop his isolated finger-movement skills as he displays each number (For example, "This Old Man, He played 1" (and so on).

Clay Writing Board

Helps your child establish an effective grasp of writing tools and builds her finger strength

What You Need

small cookie sheet or pizza pan | modeling clay (single color works best) | **stylus** (a wooden or metal tool used to make indentations in clay (available at craft stores). Make your own stylus by using a pen with the ink barrel removed or a chopstick

What to Do

- Invite your child to help you spread modeling clay evenly over the cookie sheet, so that the clay is $1/4$" or $1/2$" thick.
- Show her the stylus and explain that it is a tool that artists use to make marks in clay.
- Show her how to use the stylus to write letters or draw shapes on the "Clay Writing Board." Demonstrate how she can use her fingers to "erase" the letters in the clay by tracing them with her index finger and pressing the clay into its original flat shape.
- Encourage her to write her name, letters, or shapes in the clay. If necessary, help her by writing the letters first and then letting her trace over them with the stylus.

Cotton Swab Painting

Improves your child's grasp strength

What You Need

cotton swabs | tempera paints | shallow containers for paints | paper (no larger than 8 ½" x 11") | easel or wall for attaching paper

What to Do

● Place the paper on an easel or tape it to a wall.

● Encourage your child to use cotton swabs as paintbrushes to create a picture.

More Fun!

● Give him a very small piece of paper to create mini artwork using the cotton swabs. A 3" x 5" index card works well.

"Itsy Bitsy" Writing Utensils

Helps your child establish an appropriate grasp of writing tools

What You Need

golf pencils or small pencils that are less than 3" in length | pieces of crayons less than 3" in length | storage containers for pencils and crayons

What to Do

- Label storage containers for golf pencils and pieces of crayons as "Itsy Bitsy."
- Give your child "Itsy Bitsy" pencils and crayons for writing and drawing.
- Encourage her to use the "Itsy Bitsy" writing utensils in different activities.

More Fun!

- Provide small pieces of chalk for the child to practice writing and drawing on sidewalks or chalk boards.
- Read a book or tell a story about a small person or animal who was "Itsy Bitsy." One favorite is "The Itsy Bitsy Spider."

Water Droppers

Increases your child's finger strength and improves his grasp of tools and utensils

What You Need

containers of water for filling eyedropper | eyedropper or **pipette** | pennies and quarters | newspaper or plastic to protect table from water spills

What to Do

- Show your child how to fill up an eyedropper with water. Then, show him how to squeeze it gently to make drips of water.
- Give him a penny and a quarter. Ask him to predict how many drops of water each coin will hold.
- Ask him to drip water slowly onto the face of each coin to see how many water drops each coin can hold. Help him count, if necessary.
- Compare results by asking questions, such as, "How many water drops did the penny hold?" "How much did the quarter hold?" "Which coin held more water drops?" "Why?"

More Fun!

- Add a few drops of dishwashing liquid to the water container. Repeat the experiment. The dishwashing liquid reduces the surface tension of the water so the coins will not hold water drops.

Coin Match

*Develops your child's eye-hand coordination
and in-hand manipulation skills*

What You Need

variety of coins, including pennies, nickels, and quarters | small bowls or plastic
containers for coins | paper | black pen or marker

What to Do

- Trace around different-sized coins to make patterns. Keep the pattern very
  simple, such as quarter, penny, quarter, penny; or nickel, nickel, penny, nickel,
  nickel, penny. Trace no more than 10 coins on each piece of paper.
- Invite your child to sort pennies, nickels and quarters, and place them in
  separate containers.
- Give her a coin pattern to replicate.
- Encourage her to select coins from the pre-sorted bowls and match them to
  their corresponding spots by size.
- When she finishes, place one coin into each container, and then ask your
  child to sort the coins back into the proper containers.

More Fun!

- Create more patterns by tracing around different coins on paper, or you
  can make coin rubbings rather than tracing around the circumference of
  the coins.

Piggy Banks

Develops your child's ability to manipulate small objects in his hand, insert small objects into a small container, and consistently use a pincer grasp to place small objects

What You Need

A piggy bank or clear, plastic jar with lid | square piece of foam at least 1" thick
sharp knife or X-ACTO™ knife (adult-use only) | variety of coins, including pennies, nickels, dimes, and quarters

Preparation (adult only)
- To make a piggy bank, wash and remove the label from the plastic jar so that it is completely transparent. Cut a slit in the jar lid. The slit must be large enough to place a quarter through it.
- To make a coin holder, cut slits in the top of the foam. The slits must be wide enough and deep enough to hold quarters. Coins should sit slightly above the foam so that your child can remove them with his fingertips.

What to Do
- Place a variety of coins flat on a table or other hard surface.
- Encourage your child to fill up the piggy bank or coin holder with coins.

More Fun!
- Make this a game and see how many coins he can put in the bank or holder in one minute. Help him count the coins while putting them inside or when he finishes.

Furry Letters

Helps your child use her in-hand manipulation skills in play and to recognize and form letters of the alphabet

What You Need

chenille sticks | 3" x 5" or 5 x 7" index cards, heavy paper, or card stock | marker | scissors (adult-use only)

What to Do

- On each card, write a letter large enough to use as a pattern for chenille sticks (adult only).
- Cut several of the chenille sticks in half; also cut some into fourths (adult only). Make three sizes of chenille sticks (whole, ¹/₂, ¹/₄).
- Show your child how to create a letter by bending the chenille to follow the pattern on the cards.
- Encourage her to make "Furry Letters" that spell her name or other words of interest.

More Fun!

- Glue the "Furry Letter Names/Words" onto heavy paper.
- Play a game with the "Furry Letters." Place the letters in a shoebox or storage container. Your child closes her eyes, reaches into the box, and pulls out a letter. See if she can identify the letter by touch.

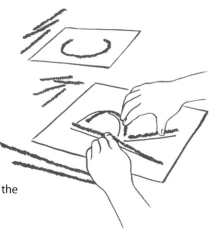

Glitter Letters

Develops your child's eye-hand coordination and gives him experience with letters

What You Need

construction paper | marker | glue | small bowls or containers | cotton swabs or craft sticks | glitter (store in jars for shaking or in open containers to sprinkle with fingers) **Note**: For easy cleanup, cover the work surface with a shower curtain, newspaper, or vinyl tablecloth.

What to Do

- Use a marker to write letters or your child's name on construction paper.
- Put glue in one container and glitter in another.
- Ask your child to use a cotton swab or craft stick to trace each letter with glue.
- Encourage him either to shake glitter from a jar or to use his fingers to sprinkle glitter over each letter.
- Gently shake the completed paper to remove excess glitter, and allow the paper to dry.

More Fun!

- Once the glitter letters are dry, he can use his fingers to trace over the letters. Ask him, "How do the letters feel?"

Rainbow Letters

Gives your child practice with writing letters and holding paper in place while writing

What You Need

plain white paper | colored pencils or thin washable markers

What to Do

- Write some letters or your child's name on white paper. Space out the letters so she has plenty of room to trace around them.
- Show her how to trace around the outside of a letter, using a different color each time. When you finish, you will have a "rainbow" letter.
- Give her paper and encourage her to trace around the letters to make her own "rainbow" letters or words.

More Fun!

- Give her glitter pens or watercolor paints and small brushes so she can make "rainbow" letters with different materials.
- Suggest that she cut out her "rainbow" letters to give her practice using scissors.

Sandbox Writing

Develops your child's finger strength and his confidence in his writing ability

What You Need

shoeboxes and solid-color contact paper (red, blue, black, and green work well) |
white sand (clean and sterilized, available at home improvement stores) |
letters of the alphabet for children to use as models

What to Do

- Cover the inside bottom of a shoebox with contact paper and coat the bottom of the box with white sand until the sand is $\frac{1}{2}$" deep (adult-only step).
- Encourage your child to write letters in the "sandbox" using his index finger. If he presses his finger hard enough, he will be able to see the colored contact paper under the sand.
- Show him how to shake the sandbox gently from side to side or smooth the sand with his hand to erase his letters.

More Fun!

- Add several drops of water to the sand or mist the sand with a spray bottle to moisten it. The slight increase in resistance in the sand will build more finger strength, as he continues to form letters with his fingers.
- Provide tools such as a craft stick, drinking straw, or chopstick for him to practice writing in the sand.

Sandpaper Writing

Develops your child's grasp strength and engages her in tactile pre-writing experiences

What You Need

sandpaper of various grits (coarse, medium, and fine grit) |
plain paper (copy or drawing) | writing tools, such as golf pencils, crayons, or
thin markers | letters or words for children to copy

What to Do

- Place the plain paper on top of the sandpaper.
- Ask your child which letters or words she wants to copy.
- As she writes on the paper, the sandpaper will add extra resistance to the writing and texture to the writing experience.
- If you use different grits of sandpaper, talk about how they feel different and how the writing looks different.

More Fun!

- Set out chalk for your child to write with directly on the sandpaper. Then encourage your child to use her fingers to erase the letters.

Write a Little Note

Helps your child use a developmentally appropriate grasp of writing tools and practice using small finger movements for writing

What You Need

small sticky notes (from 1"–3" square) | golf pencils or short adult pencils (less than 3" long)

What to Do

- Give your child several sticky notes and a small pencil.
- Talk about the different "notes" that people write throughout the day, such as phone messages, "to-do" lists, wish lists, or notes to friends.
- Encourage him to write a little note and read it to you.

More Fun!

- Encourage your child to draw a "teeny tiny" picture on a sticky note. Your child can use markers or crayons to decorate several sticky notes and then stick them to a larger piece of paper to form a sticky note collage.

Make Your Own Puzzle

Encourages your child to create art using scissors

What You Need

thick paper, such as oak tag, card stock, or poster board | thin and thick markers
| child-safe scissors | resealable plastic bags

What to Do

- Give your child a piece of thick paper, no larger than 8 $\frac{1}{2}$" x 11". If you are using poster board, turn it to the non-glossy side.
- Explain how you are going to make a puzzle:
  - Use markers to draw a picture or design that will fill up the entire piece of paper.
  - Cut the picture into 8–12 puzzle pieces.
  - Put the puzzle together.
- Make sure your child uses ample color in her pictures and designs. This will make the puzzle easier to put together.
- When she has finished her picture, help her cut the paper into puzzle pieces, ensuring that the pieces are not too small to manipulate.
- Encourage her to practice putting her puzzle together.
- Store the puzzle in a resealable plastic bag and label it with a short description (for example, "my house" or "rainbow").

More Fun!

- Add small rulers and/or templates to the materials. She can use them to draw lines or make designs for her puzzles.

Animal Masks

Develops your child's ability to use scissors and gives him experience with drawing tools

What You Need

thick, white paper such as construction paper or card stock (8 ½" x 11") | variety of drawing tools such as colored pencils, thin markers, small crayons, glitter pens, or paint pens | child-safe scissors | 1-hole punch | yarn or string

What to Do

- Cut out a mask using this pattern as a guide (adult-only step).
- Ask your child to use a pencil, marker, or crayon to trace around the mask on the thick paper.
- Give him various drawing utensils to decorate the mask and create an animal face.
- Help him cut out his mask, if necessary. Be sure the eyes are well positioned so that he can see.
- Guide him as he uses the 1-hole punch to place one hole on either side of the mask.
- Tie yarn or string through the holes to fit the mask to his face.

More Fun!

- Ask him questions about the animal he has "become," such as, "What sound do you make?" or "How do you walk?"
- Act out a simple story using the mask, and make additional masks for other characters in the story.

Paper Dolls

Develops your child's eye-hand coordination and bilateral hand skills

What You Need

thick paper such as card stock or posterboard | child-safe scissors | scissors (adult-use only) | variety of paper, including paper with designs, such as scrapbook paper, greeting cards, construction paper, foil, and sandpaper | scrap materials , including yarn, beads, buttons, cotton fabric, and sequins | glue | small pieces of chalk, crayons, markers, or stubby pencils | resealable plastic storage bags

What to Do

- Cut out paper dolls using this pattern as a guide (adult-only step). The dolls should be 6"–8" long (see next page for pattern).
- Give your child a variety of materials and glue to decorate the dolls.
- Suggest that she add faces and hair to her dolls using glue, yarn, beads, buttons, crayons, and markers. Allow the dolls to dry.
- Remove the glue from the work area, and give her various pieces of paper and cotton fabric.
- Talk about how to make clothes for her dolls. She can make several different clothing items to dress her dolls.
- Encourage your child to use the chalk, crayons, markers, or pencils to draw patterns for the doll's clothing. Demonstrate how to trace around the dolls on the paper or fabric. Cut out the clothing.
- Invite her to dress her dolls by placing the dolls flat on the tabletop and covering them with the clothing cutouts. It's best not to glue the clothing to the dolls so that she can change their outfits.

Paper Mobile

Develops your child's scissor skills and eye-hand coordination

What You Need

thin paper (cut in squares) in solid colors, such as copy paper, tracing paper, or wrapping paper | pencils and child-safe scissors

What to Do

- Cut paper into 6" x 6" or 8" x 8" squares (adult-only step).
- Model for your child how to fold his piece of paper (assist as necessary).
  - Fold the paper in half, with opposite corners touching, to form a triangle.
  - Fold the paper in half again, to form a smaller triangle.
  - Draw alternating lines, about ½" apart on paper triangle, as shown in the illustration (adult-only step). Encourage your child to cut directly on the lines, making sure not to cut all the way across the paper.
  - Gently open the paper to form a "Paper Mobile."

More Fun!

- Staple a string to the top of the mobile to hang it.
- Staple two "Paper Mobiles" together at each corner and then gently pull apart to make accordion-like paper art.

Snowflakes

Helps your child learn to coordinate use of two hands in play

What You Need

white paper (cut into squares) that is good for folding, such as copy paper or drawing paper | child-safe scissors

What to Do

- Cut pieces of paper into 4" x 4" to 8" x 8" squares (adult-only step).
- Demonstrate the following method for folding paper and help your child, as needed. Draw lines on the paper to help her know where to fold.

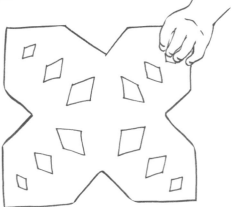

- Fold the paper in half, with opposite corners touching, to form a triangle.
- Fold the paper in half again, to form a smaller triangle.
- Show her a method for snipping or cutting the edges of the paper triangle.
- Open the paper to reveal a snowflake.
- Use waxed paper or foil wrapping paper to make unusual snowflakes.
- Give her glitter glue and sparkles to decorate her snowflakes.

Lace Up Those Shoes

Develops your child's lacing and tying skills, self-care skills, and eye-hand coordination

What You Need

variety of adult or large children's shoes that lace, such as tennis shoes, dress shoes, boots, or unusual shoes | various shoelaces with good tips, including leather, fabric, and elastic

What to Do

- Remove the laces from several pairs of shoes (adult-only step).
- Challenge your child to pair up the shoes with the correct laces.
- Show him how to lace the shoes, using verbal directions, such as:
  - Start at the two holes near the toe of the shoe.
  - Pull the shoelace through each hole until the two sides of the lace are equal.
  - String the lace through each hole.
- Help him hold a shoe in his lap or put the shoe on his foot.
- Watch him lace and tie the shoes and help him as needed
- After he finishes lacing his shoes, encourage him to put on a fashion show and walk around in the shoes he laced.

More Fun!

- There are various ways to lace shoes. Encourage your child to make his own lacing patterns.

Clay Sculptures: Self-Portrait

Improves your child's hand skills and gives her a chance to experiment with a variety of tools in play

What You Need

modeling clay | wax paper | variety of tools, including rolling pins, stylus (piece of wood shaped like a pencil for carving clay), craft sticks, toothpicks, child-safe scissors, plastic knives, and small mallets | mirror(s) (hand-held or standing) | air-tight storage containers

What to Do

- Talk with your child about how artists make sculptures. Go to your local library and ask the librarian to help you find books about sculptors, both classic and modern, for example: Michaelangelo, Rodin, Henry Moore, Alexander Calder, and Ruth Asawa. Share these books with your child.
- Place a piece of modeling clay on wax paper, and show her the various tools she can use to create her sculpture.
- Encourage her to make a self-portrait.
- Suggest that she look at herself in the mirror before and during the process.
- This project may continue over several days. Store the clay in air-tight containers overnight, or cover the sculptures with moist towels so that the clay does not harden. Resealable plastic bags or plastic wrap also work.

Magic Rocket

Develops your child's confidence in using his
hands to construct objects

What You Need

paper towel rolls | wrapping paper rolls | paper plates | child-safe scissors
| tape (masking, duct, or electrical) | construction paper | various materials
for decorating (markers, crayons, star stickers, or paint)

What to Do

- Set out the materials on a work surface.
- Show your child a picture or read a book about a rocket or spaceship. Two good choices are *Roaring Rockets (Amazing Machines)* by Tony Mitton and Ant Parker and *On the Launch Pad: A Counting Book about Rockets* by Michael Dahl.
- Encourage your child to build his own "Magic Rocket" by taping materials together. Paper plates can be cut in half to make wings or a propeller. Use the construction paper to make a cone-shaped tip of the rocket ship.
- Help by holding materials or cutting tape, as needed.
- Once he finishes constructing his "Magic Rocket," he can decorate it with markers, crayons, or paint.

More Fun!

- Create a telescope. Tape two or three paper towel rolls end to end to form a long telescope.
- Create binoculars. Cut a paper towel roll in half. Tape the two parts side to side to form binoculars.

Nature Prints

Develops your child's ability to grasp tools effectively

What You Need

collection of objects from outdoors (flat objects with texture work best) such as leaves, bark, grass, flowers, rocks, or shells | thin, white paper such as typing, tracing, or onionskin paper | small crayons and pieces of crayons

What to Do

- Talk to your child about print making.
- Show her the method of print making by placing a flat object under a piece of paper, and use a piece of crayon to rub across the paper.
- Discuss the collection of nature items.
- Encourage her to explore the objects and make her own prints.

More Fun!

- Talk to your child about some of the reasons why certain objects do not make a print. Encourage your child to collect items from around the room to discover if they will make a print.

Off to Work I Go!

Develops your child's small muscle dexterity and eye-hand coordination and gives him confidence in his fine motor abilities

What You Need

briefcase or messenger bag | paper used at work, such as address books, notepads, sticky notes, and memo pads | variety of writing utensils, such as pencils, thin markers, and washable pens | 1-hole punch, ruler, tape, and glue sticks | cell phone (play or non-functioning) | calculator

What to Do

- Create a briefcase for your child.
- Talk to your child about the function of a briefcase and the things that are found inside it.
- He can explore the briefcase and use the tools in play.

More Fun!

- Put a wallet or coin purse with coins inside the briefcase to add another level of learning and imaginative play.

Painted Flower Pots

Helps your child manipulate tools in play, learn to create art with a variety of materials, and use an effective grasp of tools

What You Need

terra cotta flowerpots | acrylic paints | small paintbrushes | foam stamps | clear acrylic spray | vinyl tablecloth, shower curtain, or newspaper to keep work surface clean | paint shirts for children

What to Do

- Give your child a flowerpot and set out the decorative materials. Invite her to decorate it.
- Spray the painted pot with clear acrylic spray (adult-only step) and allow it to dry.

More Fun!

- Fill the pot with a flower or plant or ask your child if she would like to make "Paper Flowers" to place inside (see page 91).

Treasure Box

Strengthens your child's grasp

What You Need

jewelry boxes or small boxes with lids | various small items for decorating boxes such as sequins, tiny beads, and buttons | small paintbrushes or cotton swabs | glue | coins

What to Do

- Encourage your child to use paintbrushes or cotton swabs to paint his treasure box with glue.
- After he finishes painting it, he can decorate it.
- Separate the box lid and bottom to let them dry separately.
- When the box and lid are dry, put the lid back on the box, and then give your child several coins to place in the box.
- Tell him to "bury the treasure" by hiding the treasure box somewhere in the room or nearby outside. You become a treasure hunter as you try to find the buried treasure.
- Take turns hiding the box and searching for it.

More Fun!

- Provide paper and markers or pencils for him to draw "treasure maps" to help the treasure hunter find the hidden treasure.

When should my child use an adult-like grasp of the pencil?

The majority of children between the ages of 4 ½ and 6 years will use a mature grasp of writing utensils. This adult-like grasp typically means that your child holds the pencil with her fingertips and has good control of the pencil. Your child's grasp will be influenced by a variety of things such as experience, eye-hand coordination, and muscle tone.

What is the best type of pencil grasp for my preschooler to use?

Typically, three-year-old children will use a **digital pronate grasp** (held with fingers; wrist straight; forearm moves with hand) OR a **static tripod posture** (held with thumb, index, and middle fingers in crude manner; ring and pinky fingers are slightly bent; held high up on pencil). Either of these grasps will work effectively for a three-year-old child who is gaining experience holding writing utensils.

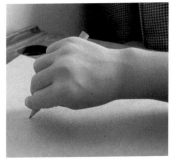

Digital pronate grasp

There are several grasps that are considered efficient (most effective) for four- and five-year-olds. These grasps include two main components:

Static tripod grasp

1. Fingertips on the end of the pencil.
2. An open space between the thumb and fingers (thumb and fingers form a circular position, so that you can see the palm of the hand).

Many children prefer to use a **dynamic tripod grasp**, holding the writing utensil between the thumb, index, and middle fingers. A **quadripod grasp** that incorporates the thumb, index, middle, and ring fingers is another effective and commonly used grasp.

Dynamic tripod grasp

When should my child be able to tie his shoes?

Most children learn to tie their shoes sometime during kindergarten. At this time, a child will usually have the bilateral hand skills, grasp, and eye-hand coordination necessary to complete this complex self-help skill. A child who wears primarily slip-on or Velcro-closure shoes will lack the experience with tying shoes and may develop this skill later.

Quadripod grasp

When should my child be able to write her name?

Many five-year-olds are able to write their first names independently. Most children learn to write their names in uppercase letters before lowercase letters. Some five-year-olds will also be able to write a few letters that are not in their first names, but which the children find interesting (for example, "M," "O," "M").

What if my preschooler writes his name backwards?

It is typical for preschoolers to write letters backwards or to orient their names backwards across the page. This is an appropriate step for young children during the learning process. Many children demonstrate letter reversals up until the end of first grade. Four- and five-year-olds need opportunities to observe, imitate, and copy letters and words in a literacy-rich environment that includes books, signs, labels, and other reading materials.

If my preschooler holds her pencil awkwardly, should I try to change her grasp?

It is important first to consider your child's age and developmental level. It would not be uncommon for a young, inexperienced preschooler to use what may look like an awkward grasp of a pencil. Young preschoolers may also grasp a pencil in a different way each time they hold one. Grasp is based on habit. So, whatever grasp the child consistently uses in later preschool and kindergarten will probably be the grasp she uses into adulthood. Make sure your child is using the appropriate size pencil. If your four- or five-year-old child consistently holds utensils with an awkward and inappropriate grasp, demonstrate the proper way to grasp a writing tool and gently reposition the pencil in the child's hand. You could try introducing your child to a pencil grip (such as a triangle-shaped grip) to help her learn to hold the pencil more appropriately.

What if my preschooler holds his scissors upside down?

It is typical for two- and three-year-olds to hold scissors upside down. Preschoolers often use this pattern if they have not had enough experience with pre-scissor activities. Provide your child with pre-scissor activities, such as picking up objects with tongs, squeezing water through turkey basters, or using a hole-punch on paper. Be sure to model the proper way to hold scissors and you may give "thumb on top" verbal reminders. With enough practice, your preschooler will develop the next stage of scissor use—holding the scissors appropriately and snipping paper.

When is it appropriate to begin teaching my child how to write the letters of the alphabet?

Children should be able to copy simple lines, shapes, and their first names before practicing the proper formation of uppercase and lowercase letters of the alphabet. Most children are not developmentally ready to begin handwriting instruction until the second half of kindergarten. Your child should not use handwriting workbook pages. Instead, provide your child with a variety of materials that include the alphabet and words, so that she has something to copy, if she so desires. You may begin by selecting a simple word or words that are interesting for your child such as "dog" or "love."

What type of paper is appropriate for my preschooler to use when writing?

Preschoolers should write on plain paper with no lines. Most four- and five-year-olds do not have the visual perceptual skills or the fine motor control necessary to write letters accurately on a line or between two lines. Elementary paper that includes the dotted line in the middle of two solid lines is even more visually confusing than wide-ruled paper, and so it is best not to use it at all during the preschool years.

What if my child is using fine motor skills that I feel are well below age-appropriate level?

If you are concerned about your child's participation in fine motor activities, you should discuss your concerns with your child's pediatrician. You may contact your local school system's **Child Find Program** or Special Education Program to request an evaluation. Your child should receive an occupational therapy evaluation to assess thoroughly his fine motor abilities. An occupational therapist (OT) who specializes in fine motor development can make recommendations for you to use at home and can also provide fine motor intervention for your preschooler.

Glossary

Bilateral Hand Skills: The ability to use both hands together to accomplish a task.

Child Find Program: A publicly-funded program under the Individuals with Disabilities Education Act (IDEA) intended to identify, locate, and evaluate/assess infants and toddlers with potential developmental delays or disabilities.

Cognitive Development: The process of thinking, learning, perception, and reasoning.

Developmentally Appropriate: Activities and educational experiences that match the child's age and stage of development.

Digital Pronate Grasp: Object is held with all fingers, wrist straight, and forearm moves with hand. Typical grasp for 2- to 3-year-olds.

Dynamic Tripod Grasp: Object is held with fingertips of thumb, index, and middle fingers; ring and little fingers bent; hand moves separately from forearm. Typical grasp for 4½- to 6-year-olds. Mature grasp pattern.

Eye-Hand Coordination: The ability to use fine motor skills to accomplish a task that the eyes and brain want to complete.

Fine Motor: Movement of the small muscles in the fingers, hands, and forearms (for example, writing, cutting with scissors, stringing beads, or drawing). Another term for "small motor."

Finger Isolation: Using one finger (for example, pointing).

Grasp: Hold with fingers.

Gross Motor Skills: Movement of the large muscles in the arms, legs, and back (for example, walking, running, or kicking). Another term for "large motor."

Hand Dominance/Handedness: The hand that develops strength, skill, and precision to perform fine motor tasks. A preference for using one hand over the other.

In-Hand Manipulation: Adjustment of object in the hand, after grasp.

Occupational Therapist (OT): A healthcare professional who helps persons overcome physical or social problems due to illness or disability. OTs are skilled in adapting the environment so that a child can participate in the occupations of childhood: play, school, and self-care.

Open-Ended Activities: Materials or projects used to create without fixed limits or restrictions. For example, drawing on a blank sheet of paper rather than a coloring book.

Pencil Grasp: How a person holds a writing tool.

Pencil Grip: Tool added to pencil to help correct an ineffective pencil grasp.

Pincer Grasp: Using index finger and thumb to hold an object.

Pipette: A syringe-like device used to pick up and dispense a liquid.

Proprioceptive Sense (Proprioception): The unconscious awareness of sensations coming from the muscles and joints that provides information about where each part of the body is and how it is moving.

Quadripod Grasp: Held with fingertips of thumb, index, middle, and ring fingers; little finger bent; hand moves separately from forearm. Mature grasp pattern.

Reciprocal Hand Skills: Using one hand to do one thing while the other hand does something different. For example, when cutting with scissors, one hand holds the paper and the other hand manipulates the scissors.

Release: Using fingers to let go of an object.

Static Tripod Grasp: Held with crude approximation of thumb, index, and middle fingers; ring and little fingers are only slightly bent; grasped high on the utensil. Typical grasp for 3½- to 4-year-olds.

Stylus: A pointed metal or wooden tool used to make indentations in the support surface.

Tactile Sense: The sensory system responsible for identifying touch input, understanding what has been felt, and preparing for a response.

Index